This Book is a Brain Dump of ...

_____

Thanks for Picking Up this Note Book.

This is Not Just an other Ordinary Idea Book. Its designed to help you capture every minute detail about your business idea. You can dump everything about your idea into a structured format that, you can refer any time in the future. Thus the name *'Beyond Just Ideas'*

It contains prompts/guidelines to help you capture the most important aspects to take your idea from just an Idea to Implementation.

During the process of journaling, you will able to Brainstorm your idea by answering to various questions like,

What Is Your Idea?
What are You Solving with your idea ?
What are challenges with current system?
Who's Your Audience?
What are Pros & Cons of your idea?
What is the Minimum Valuable Product for your Idea?
What challenges you foresee during implementation?
What are the Resources available?

You've also got space to take Notes & Draw the concept or workflow of your idea or business plan, which is aimed to help you declutter your mind from the Creative Thoughts.

Copyright © 2019 All rights reserved. No portion of this book may be reproduced in any form without permission from the publisher, except as permitted by copyright law.

Idea #	Your Idea	Page #
Idea # 1	_____	___
Idea # 2	_____	___
Idea # 3	_____	___
Idea # 4	_____	___
Idea # 5	_____	___
Idea # 6	_____	___
Idea # 7	_____	___
Idea # 8	_____	___
Idea # 9	_____	___
Idea # 10	_____	___
Idea # 11	_____	___
Idea # 12	_____	___
Idea # 13	_____	___
Idea # 14	_____	___
Idea # 15	_____	___

_____

Write your idea in one line. May it be the name or your idea/product/concept.

Describe Your Idea

Detail out complete information about your idea. Your concept, solution, etc.,

What are we solving?

Define the problem statement here. What are the challenges with existing system (if any).

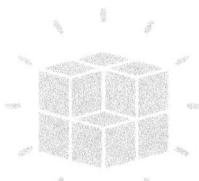

Who is Our Audience?

Define who your customers/audience are. You can also consider your typical customer persona, to give you an idea about who you are targeting this idea for.

Draw Your Concept

Draw a sketch of your implementation plan or workflow to get your idea productized.

Define Your MVP

What is your Minimum Valuable Product to create and make it available for public.

Foreseen Challenges & Mitigation Plans

Note down the challenges that may come across, that you already are aware of.

Resources

List out all the resources that can help you on this idea.

Other Notes

Space for any notes that you can think of.

Other Notes

Space for any notes that you can think of.

Other Notes

Space for any notes that you can think of.

_____

Write your idea in one line. May it be the name or your idea/product/concept.

Describe Your Idea

Detail out complete information about your idea. Your concept, solution, etc.,

What are we solving?

Define the problem statement here. What are the challenges with existing system (if any).

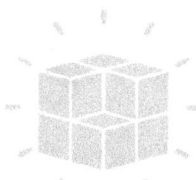

Who is Our Audience?

Define who your customers/audience are. You can also consider your typical customer persona, to give you an idea about who you are targeting this idea for.

Pros
List down all Pros of your idea.

Cons
List down all Cons of your idea.

Implementation Plan
Write down, how you plan to implement your idea & Your Projected Timelines.
Outsourcing, Hiring, Kickstarter Campaigning, etc.,

Draw Your Concept

Draw a sketch of your implementation plan or workflow to get your idea productized.

Define Your MVP

What is your Minimum Valuable Product to create and make it available for public.

Foreseen Challenges & Mitigation Plans

Note down the challenges that may come across, that you already are aware of.

Resources

List out all the resources that can help you on this idea.

Other Notes

Space for any notes that you can think of.

Other Notes

Space for any notes that you can think of.

Other Notes

Space for any notes that you can think of.

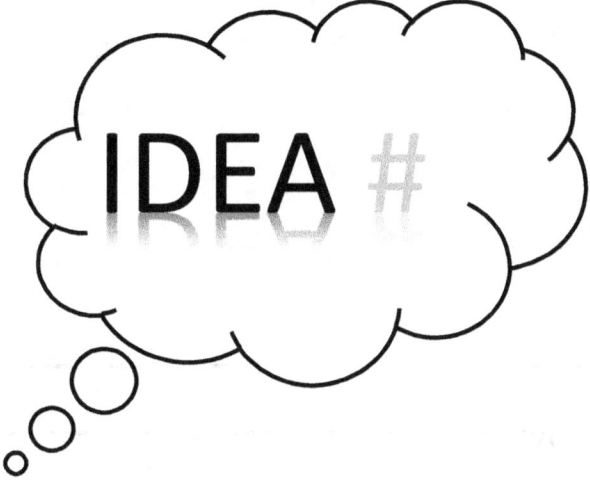

_____

Write your idea in one line. May it be the name or your idea/product/concept.

Describe Your Idea

Detail out complete information about your idea. Your concept, solution, etc.,

What are we solving?

Define the problem statement here. What are the challenges with existing system (if any).

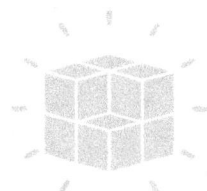

Who is Our Audience?

Define who your customers/audience are. You can also consider your typical customer persona, to give you an idea about who you are targeting this idea for.

Pros
List down all Pros of your idea.

Cons
List down all Cons of your idea.

Implementation Plan
Write down, how you plan to implement your idea & Your Projected Timelines.
Outsourcing, Hiring, Kickstarter Campaigning, etc.,

Draw Your Concept

Draw a sketch of your implementation plan or workflow to get your idea productized.

Define Your MVP

What is your Minimum Valuable Product to create and make it available for public.

Foreseen Challenges & Mitigation Plans

Note down the challenges that may come across, that you already are aware of.

Resources

List out all the resources that can help you on this idea.

Other Notes

Space for any notes that you can think of.

Other Notes

Space for any notes that you can think of.

Other Notes

Space for any notes that you can think of.

_____

Write your idea in one line. May it be the name or your idea/product/concept.

Describe Your Idea

Detail out complete information about your idea. Your concept, solution, etc.,

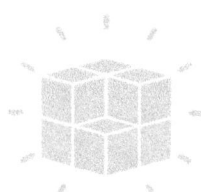

What are we solving?

Define the problem statement here. What are the challenges with existing system (if any).

Who is Our Audience?

Define who your customers/audience are. You can also consider your typical customer persona, to give you an idea about who you are targeting this idea for.

Pros

List down all Pros of your idea.

Cons

List down all Cons of your idea.

Implementation Plan

Write down, how you plan to implement your idea & Your Projected Timelines.
Outsourcing, Hiring, Kickstarter Campaigning, etc.,

Draw Your Concept

Draw a sketch of your implementation plan or workflow to get your idea productized.

Define Your MVP

What is your Minimum Valuable Product to create and make it available for public.

Foreseen Challenges & Mitigation Plans

Note down the challenges that may come across, that you already are aware of.

Resources

List out all the resources that can help you on this idea.

Other Notes

Space for any notes that you can think of.

Other Notes

Space for any notes that you can think of.

Other Notes

Space for any notes that you can think of.

_____

Write your idea in one line. May it be the name or your idea/product/concept.

Describe Your Idea

Detail out complete information about your idea. Your concept, solution, etc.,

What are we solving?

Define the problem statement here. What are the challenges with existing system (if any).

Who is Our Audience?

Define who your customers/audience are. You can also consider your typical customer persona, to give you an idea about who you are targeting this idea for.

Pros

List down all Pros of your idea.

Cons

List down all Cons of your idea.

Implementation Plan

Write down, how you plan to implement your idea & Your Projected Timelines.
Outsourcing, Hiring, Kickstarter Campaigning, etc.,

Draw Your Concept

Draw a sketch of your implementation plan or workflow to get your idea productized.

Define Your MVP

What is your Minimum Valuable Product to create and make it available for public.

Foreseen Challenges & Mitigation Plans

Note down the challenges that may come across, that you already are aware of.

Resources

List out all the resources that can help you on this idea.

Other Notes

Space for any notes that you can think of.

Other Notes

Space for any notes that you can think of.

Other Notes

Space for any notes that you can think of.

_____

Write your idea in one line. May it be the name or your idea/product/concept.

Describe Your Idea

Detail out complete information about your idea. Your concept, solution, etc.,

What are we solving?

Define the problem statement here. What are the challenges with existing system (if any).

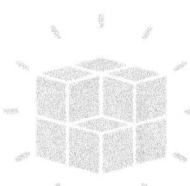

Who is Our Audience?

Define who your customers/audience are. You can also consider your typical customer persona, to give you an idea about who you are targeting this idea for.

Pros

List down all Pros of your idea.

Cons

List down all Cons of your idea.

Implementation Plan

Write down, how you plan to implement your idea & Your Projected Timelines.
Outsourcing, Hiring, Kickstarter Campaigning, etc.,

Draw Your Concept

Draw a sketch of your implementation plan or workflow to get your idea productized.

Define Your MVP

What is your Minimum Valuable Product to create and make it available for public.

Foreseen Challenges & Mitigation Plans

Note down the challenges that may come across, that you already are aware of.

Resources

List out all the resources that can help you on this idea.

Other Notes

Space for any notes that you can think of.

Other Notes

Space for any notes that you can think of.

Other Notes

Space for any notes that you can think of.

_____

Write your idea in one line. May it be the name or your idea/product/concept.

Describe Your Idea
Detail out complete information about your idea. Your concept, solution, etc.,

What are we solving?
Define the problem statement here. What are the challenges with existing system (if any).

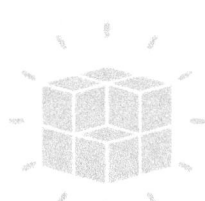

Who is Our Audience?
Define who your customers/audience are. You can also consider your typical customer persona, to give you an idea about who you are targeting this idea for.

Pros

List down all Pros of your idea.

Cons

List down all Cons of your idea.

Implementation Plan

Write down, how you plan to implement your idea & Your Projected Timelines.
Outsourcing, Hiring, Kickstarter Campaigning, etc.,

Draw Your Concept

Draw a sketch of your implementation plan or workflow to get your idea productized.

Define Your MVP

What is your Minimum Valuable Product to create and make it available for public.

Foreseen Challenges & Mitigation Plans

Note down the challenges that may come across, that you already are aware of.

Resources

List out all the resources that can help you on this idea.

Other Notes

Space for any notes that you can think of.

Other Notes

Space for any notes that you can think of.

Other Notes

Space for any notes that you can think of.

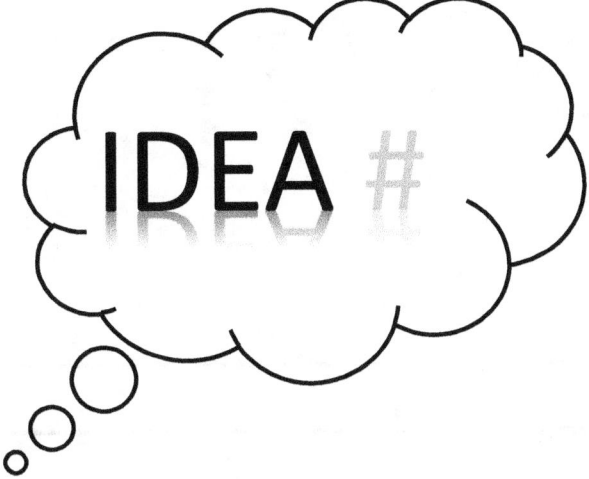

_____

Write your idea in one line. May it be the name or your idea/product/concept.

Describe Your Idea

Detail out complete information about your idea. Your concept, solution, etc.,

What are we solving?

Define the problem statement here. What are the challenges with existing system (if any).

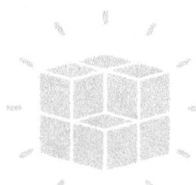

Who is Our Audience?

Define who your customers/audience are. You can also consider your typical customer persona, to give you an idea about who you are targeting this idea for.

Pros
List down all Pros of your idea.

Cons
List down all Cons of your idea.

Implementation Plan
Write down, how you plan to implement your idea & Your Projected Timelines.
Outsourcing, Hiring, Kickstarter Campaigning, etc.,

Draw Your Concept

Draw a sketch of your implementation plan or workflow to get your idea productized.

Define Your MVP

What is your Minimum Valuable Product to create and make it available for public.

Foreseen Challenges & Mitigation Plans

Note down the challenges that may come across, that you already are aware of.

Resources

List out all the resources that can help you on this idea.

Other Notes

Space for any notes that you can think of.

Other Notes

Space for any notes that you can think of.

Other Notes

Space for any notes that you can think of.

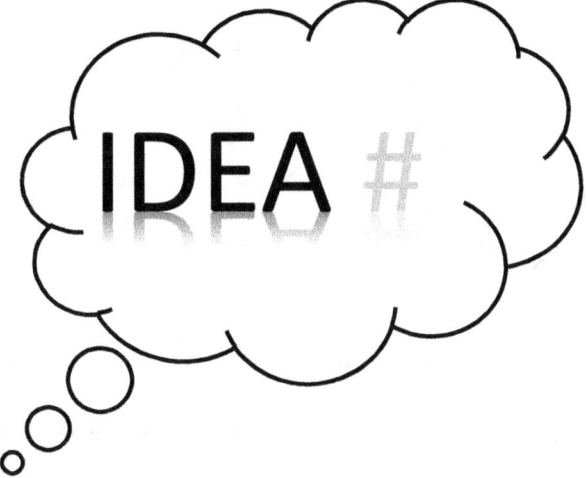

_____

Write your idea in one line. May it be the name or your idea/product/concept.

Describe Your Idea

Detail out complete information about your idea. Your concept, solution, etc.,

What are we solving?

Define the problem statement here. What are the challenges with existing system (if any).

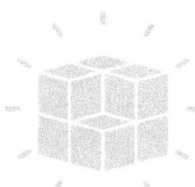

Who is Our Audience?

Define who your customers/audience are. You can also consider your typical customer persona, to give you an idea about who you are targeting this idea for.

Pros

List down all Pros of your idea.

Cons

List down all Cons of your idea.

Implementation Plan

Write down, how you plan to implement your idea & Your Projected Timelines.
Outsourcing, Hiring, Kickstarter Campaigning, etc.,

Draw Your Concept

Draw a sketch of your implementation plan or workflow to get your idea productized.

Define Your MVP

What is your Minimum Valuable Product to create and make it available for public.

Foreseen Challenges & Mitigation Plans

Note down the challenges that may come across, that you already are aware of.

Resources

List out all the resources that can help you on this idea.

Other Notes

Space for any notes that you can think of.

Other Notes

Space for any notes that you can think of.

Other Notes

Space for any notes that you can think of.

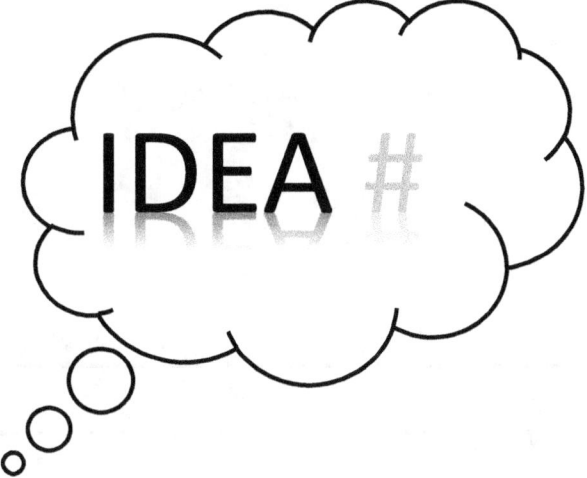

_____

Write your idea in one line. May it be the name or your idea/product/concept.

Describe Your Idea

Detail out complete information about your idea. Your concept, solution, etc.,

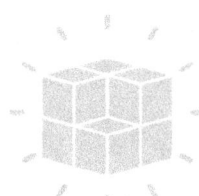

What are we solving?

Define the problem statement here. What are the challenges with existing system (if any).

Who is Our Audience?

Define who your customers/audience are. You can also consider your typical customer persona, to give you an idea about who you are targeting this idea for.

Pros

List down all Pros of your idea.

Cons

List down all Cons of your idea.

Implementation Plan

Write down, how you plan to implement your idea & Your Projected Timelines.
Outsourcing, Hiring, Kickstarter Campaigning, etc.,

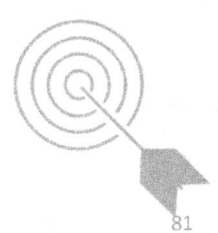

Draw Your Concept

Draw a sketch of your implementation plan or workflow to get your idea productized.

Define Your MVP

What is your Minimum Valuable Product to create and make it available for public.

Foreseen Challenges & Mitigation Plans

Note down the challenges that may come across, that you already are aware of.

Resources

List out all the resources that can help you on this idea.

Other Notes

Space for any notes that you can think of.

Other Notes

Space for any notes that you can think of.

Other Notes

Space for any notes that you can think of.

_____

Write your idea in one line. May it be the name or your idea/product/concept.

Describe Your Idea

Detail out complete information about your idea. Your concept, solution, etc.,

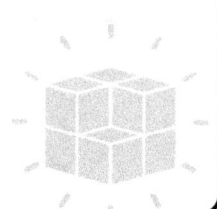

What are we solving?

Define the problem statement here. What are the challenges with existing system (if any).

Who is Our Audience?

Define who your customers/audience are. You can also consider your typical customer persona, to give you an idea about who you are targeting this idea for.

Pros

List down all Pros of your idea.

Cons

List down all Cons of your idea.

Implementation Plan

Write down, how you plan to implement your idea & Your Projected Timelines.
Outsourcing, Hiring, Kickstarter Campaigning, etc.,

Draw Your Concept

Draw a sketch of your implementation plan or workflow to get your idea productized.

Define Your MVP

What is your Minimum Valuable Product to create and make it available for public.

Foreseen Challenges & Mitigation Plans

Note down the challenges that may come across, that you already are aware of.

Resources

List out all the resources that can help you on this idea.

Other Notes

Space for any notes that you can think of.

Other Notes

Space for any notes that you can think of.

Other Notes

Space for any notes that you can think of.

_____

Write your idea in one line. May it be the name or your idea/product/concept.

Describe Your Idea

Detail out complete information about your idea. Your concept, solution, etc.,

What are we solving?

Define the problem statement here. What are the challenges with existing system (if any).

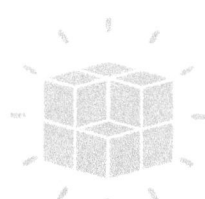

Who is Our Audience?

Define who your customers/audience are. You can also consider your typical customer persona, to give you an idea about who you are targeting this idea for.

Pros

List down all Pros of your idea.

Cons

List down all Cons of your idea.

Implementation Plan

Write down, how you plan to implement your idea & Your Projected Timelines.
Outsourcing, Hiring, Kickstarter Campaigning, etc.,

Draw Your Concept

Draw a sketch of your implementation plan or workflow to get your idea productized.

Define Your MVP

What is your Minimum Valuable Product to create and make it available for public.

Foreseen Challenges & Mitigation Plans

Note down the challenges that may come across, that you already are aware of.

Resources

List out all the resources that can help you on this idea.

Other Notes

Space for any notes that you can think of.

Other Notes

Space for any notes that you can think of.

Other Notes

Space for any notes that you can think of.

_____

Write your idea in one line. May it be the name or your idea/product/concept.

Describe Your Idea

Detail out complete information about your idea. Your concept, solution, etc.,

What are we solving?

Define the problem statement here. What are the challenges with existing system (if any).

Who is Our Audience?

Define who your customers/audience are. You can also consider your typical customer persona, to give you an idea about who you are targeting this idea for.

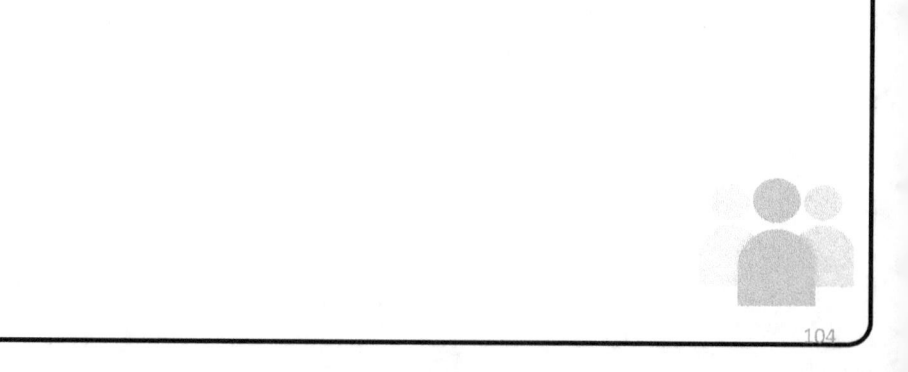

Pros
List down all Pros of your idea.

Cons
List down all Cons of your idea.

Implementation Plan
Write down, how you plan to implement your idea & Your Projected Timelines.
Outsourcing, Hiring, Kickstarter Campaigning, etc.,

Draw Your Concept

Draw a sketch of your implementation plan or workflow to get your idea productized.

Define Your MVP

What is your Minimum Valuable Product to create and make it available for public.

Foreseen Challenges & Mitigation Plans

Note down the challenges that may come across, that you already are aware of.

Resources

List out all the resources that can help you on this idea.

Other Notes

Space for any notes that you can think of.

Other Notes

Space for any notes that you can think of.

Other Notes

Space for any notes that you can think of.

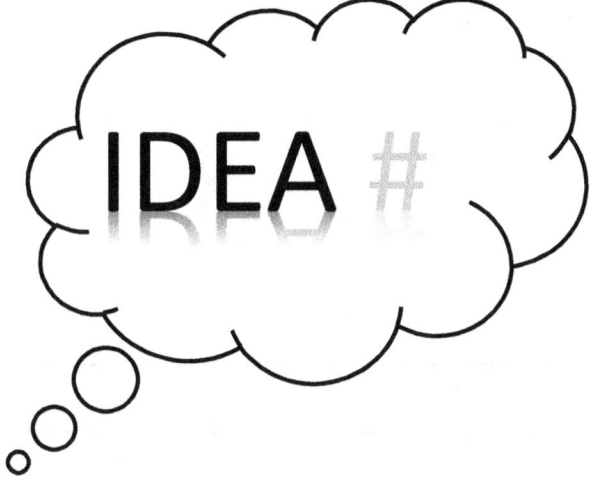

_____

Write your idea in one line. May it be the name or your idea/product/concept.

Describe Your Idea

Detail out complete information about your idea. Your concept, solution, etc.,

What are we solving?

Define the problem statement here. What are the challenges with existing system (if any).

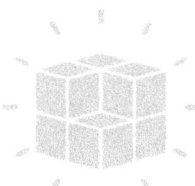

Who is Our Audience?

Define who your customers/audience are. You can also consider your typical customer persona, to give you an idea about who you are targeting this idea for.

Pros
List down all Pros of your idea.

Cons
List down all Cons of your idea.

Implementation Plan
Write down, how you plan to implement your idea & Your Projected Timelines.
Outsourcing, Hiring, Kickstarter Campaigning, etc.,

Draw Your Concept

Draw a sketch of your implementation plan or workflow to get your idea productized.

Define Your MVP

What is your Minimum Valuable Product to create and make it available for public.

Foreseen Challenges & Mitigation Plans

Note down the challenges that may come across, that you already are aware of.

Resources

List out all the resources that can help you on this idea.

Other Notes

Space for any notes that you can think of.

Other Notes

Space for any notes that you can think of.

Other Notes

Space for any notes that you can think of.

_____
Write your idea in one line. May it be the name or your idea/product/concept.

Describe Your Idea

Detail out complete information about your idea. Your concept, solution, etc.,

What are we solving?

Define the problem statement here. What are the challenges with existing system (if any).

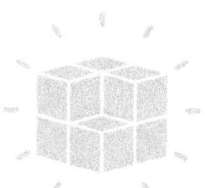

Who is Our Audience?

Define who your customers/audience are. You can also consider your typical customer persona, to give you an idea about who you are targeting this idea for.

Pros

List down all Pros of your idea.

Cons

List down all Cons of your idea.

Implementation Plan

Write down, how you plan to implement your idea & Your Projected Timelines.
Outsourcing, Hiring, Kickstarter Campaigning, etc.,

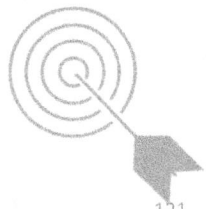

Draw Your Concept

Draw a sketch of your implementation plan or workflow to get your idea productized.

Define Your MVP

What is your Minimum Valuable Product to create and make it available for public.

Foreseen Challenges & Mitigation Plans

Note down the challenges that may come across, that you already are aware of.

Resources

List out all the resources that can help you on this idea.

Other Notes

Space for any notes that you can think of.

Other Notes

Space for any notes that you can think of.

Other Notes

Space for any notes that you can think of.

www.ingramcontent.com/pod-product-compliance
Lightning Source LLC
Chambersburg PA
CBHW080921170526
45158CB00008B/2187